KEEPING IT SIMPLE

... A Trinity ...

Emotional Healing through Meditation, the Chakras

and Psychospiritual Therapy

KEEPING IT SIMPLE

Copyright February 2011 Audrey Austin

Copyright Registration #1084355

No part of this book may be used or reproduced by any means, in whole or in part, or in any manner whatsoever including any form of electronic data retrieval system or manual copying without written permission of the author except in the case of brief quotations embodied in critical articles and reviews.

For inquiries: audrey@persona.ca

Keeping It Simple, Second Edition

ISBN-13-978-0-9780238-3-6

Cover Design & Illustrations: Susan Ruby Krupp

http://yuneekpix.com

KEEPING IT SIMPLE

"Imagine Being Whole"

by

Audrey Austin,

Psychotherapy Practitioner/Author/Teacher

TABLE OF CONTENTS

6	About the author
8	What is meditation and why do we meditate?
17	What is psychospiritual therapy?
21	What is a chakra?
28	Overview of the chakra system
33	Base Chakra
54	Meditation for Base Chakra
58	Sacral Chakra
73	Meditation for Sacral Chakra
77	Solar Plexus Chakra
104	Meditation for Solar Plexus Chakra
109	Heart Chakra

136	Meditation for Heart Chakra
140	Throat Chakra
158	Meditation for Throat Chakra
161	Brow Chakra
180	Meditation for Brow Chakra
187	Crown Chakra
195	Meditation for Crown Chakra
200	Summary

***

ABOUT THE AUTHOR

As a Psychospiritual Therapist and co-owner of Creative Connections Centre in Caledon East, it was my privilege and pleasure, in addition to carrying on a private counseling practice, to facilitate meditation and other personal growth classes in our *"One Room Schoolhouse"*.

It was not uncommon for an interested student to attend his first introductory meditation class with no prior knowledge of meditation or of the chakra system. For this reason I found it beneficial and in the highest interest of all concerned to *keep it simple.*

Simplicity in meditation, as in life, is an admirable goal. My students and I recognized as classes proceeded that it was not always easy to be simple. Life, with its myriad of challenges, has a habit of doing its best to get in the way. Nevertheless we kept our focus on this goal and felt grateful when it was achieved.

By special request of some of our Centre's students I put together some rough notes and this teaching material was utilized in class.

Since offering the Meditation Circles at Holy Trinity United Church and also the Emotional Healing Classes through Learning in Retirement in Elliot Lake, I have received requests for a book on the topic of self-discovery and personal growth. These requests have encouraged me to get to work and expand on my earlier rough notes to create this book titled <u>KEEPING IT SIMPLE</u>.

It is my highest hope that you, the reader, will find it a useful guide as you continue your journey along the path of self-discovery and personal growth.

***

WHAT IS MEDITATION

and

WHY DO WE MEDITATE?

First things first! *What is meditation?*

A form of prayer, meditation is a respecter of all religions and an integral part of most. It is a form of communication with a Higher Power that does not restrict itself to a particular faith or religion.

Yet meditation does not require the one who meditates to be affiliated with a religion.

I refer to the wisdom of the ancients. We are taught that Jesus said, *"Go into your closet and pray."* Buddha said, *"Hear the sound of one hand clapping."* Elevated psychological insights of meditation can give birth to *dviekus* meaning Cleaving to God, particularly in Jewish mysticism.

When meditating, using a mantra such as *'Om'* has a deep spiritual significance. It is representative of the conscious, unconscious and dream states of the human mind as well as symbolizing creation and the nature of *'Brahma'*, the Hindu creator-God.

At its highest level, meditation is the searcher's way of saying, *"Speak Lord, thy servant heareth."*

When one meditates the practitioner attempts to get beyond the *"thinking mind"* into a deeper state of awareness. Meditation has been practiced since antiquity and is a component of many religions but it is also practiced outside of religious traditions. Your goal may be one of many possibilities. Through meditation one can achieve a higher state of consciousness or enlightenment; develop increasing compassion and loving kindness; receive spiritual inspiration or guidance from God. You may wish to achieve greater focus, creativity or self-awareness. Another goal of meditation may be to simply cultivate a more relaxed and peaceful frame of mind.

Traditional prayer in the western world is our way of speaking to God.

Meditation is our way of listening to God. It is also our way of connecting with the divine aspect within; our highest, best selves.

Now that you have some explanation as to what meditation is, I will discuss why you may want to introduce this experience into your life and make it an implicit part of your lifestyle?

We must consider the power of prayer to answer the second question which is *why do we meditate?*

KEEPING IT SIMPLE

We are most accustomed to traditional prayer in the western world however both forms of prayer are powerful. It has been said that a good communicator will speak without offending and listen without defending. Meditation is one way of listening to your highest, most wise self and it is an enlightening way of listening to God.

Meditation is this and much more. It feeds the spirit. It nourishes body and mind. We are each comprised of body, mind and spirit. We yearn to be one, whole and complete.

Emotional blocks can get in the way and prevent us from achieving this goal and if these emotional issues are not dealt with they can manifest in physical blocks. These physical blocks or *dis-ease* can lead an individual to what is sometimes labeled a *spiritual by-pass*.

KEEPING IT SIMPLE

Perhaps you have heard the saying, *the spirit is willing but the flesh is weak.* Meditation, in and of itself, will not heal emotional and physical blocks however it will assist you in identifying these blockages. And once you have made this identification you will find yourself at a cross-road where you gain a keen awareness and a knowing that you have choice.

You can choose to ignore this new awareness or you can choose, with the assistance of a trained therapist or counselor, to deal with and work through your emotional issues. Most of us are well aware of the physical, emotional, mental and spiritual aspects of the self. Too often, we feel the separation between these aspects. We can learn that this separation is not only unnecessary but unhealthy. A new door will open and allow you to be unified in body, mind and spirit; whole and complete.

KEEPING IT SIMPLE

When you meditate you can observe your breath, your life force which is sometimes called *prana*. Breathe in relaxation and breathe out the stress and worries of the day as though they had never existed. This exercise is the foundation of all meditation. Practicing chaotic breathing will enhance insight and increase self-awareness; God awareness. Entering a doorway to conscious living; you will be able to bring the subconscious into the realm of consciousness.

It is good to be in touch with your body; to be able to hear the body's cry for relaxation, stress reduction and peace. It is possible, through meditation, to realize that you have choice. You can choose to take the steps required to meet these urgent needs.

Meditation is also a way to observe your inner self; a way to discover that you are on your way to a miracle and that, wonder of wonders, the miracle is you. Doors are opened that you may have thought were closed to you. And through these open doors you discover repressed creativity you didn't know was yours. New problem-solving abilities; enhanced insight as well as increased perception and performance are some of the gifts that will come your way.

Working with light and dark, you are given the opportunity to shine a light on those aspects of self that lurk in the shadows of your being. Your fears and losses find avenues of expression. A safe way is discovered to acknowledge and honour the grief, hurt, guilt and anger feelings that have been long repressed in the dark basement of the soul.

With the assistance of a trained therapist or counselor these repressed feelings can be felt, owned and worked through in a safe environment. There are no good or bad emotions. There are simply emotions desiring recognition, gratitude, transformation and release in a manner which will enhance the student's life. Meditation is a pathway leading to a desire for emotional, spiritual and physical healing.

Through meditation, as a willing student, you will meet your wounded inner child; that aspect of your being that survived childhood but still bears the scars and burdens of not being seen, not being heard and not being honoured for the wonderful person you truly are. A willing meditation practitioner will begin to understand that the outward manifestation of poor physical health can be transformed through understanding the spiritual, emotional blockages that were formed as necessary defenses in childhood.

There are many reasons to make meditation a part of your lifestyle. Support, wisdom and love are there in a heartbeat and through meditation you will learn that you are never alone. Having said all this, I remind myself to keep it simple. Meditation is a

KEEPING IT SIMPLE

pathway to an overall sense of well-being; physical, mental, emotional and spiritual.

***

WHAT IS PSYCHOSPIRITUAL THERAPY?

It is my personal belief that when a child is born, that tiny baby is pure and wonderful essence. This child then begins a journey called *life*. As a child strives to learn about her surroundings, her body, her care-givers, her society and her new world, she discovers she has to adjust to protect the pure and wonderful essence she truly is.

And so it is for every child; so it is for me and for you.

To protect this beautiful essence, in our childhood cleverness, we build layers around it. Every time we are shamed we build another layer. Every time we are angry and not allowed to express anger in a healthy way, we build another layer. Every time we feel guilt, we put up yet another layer of protection around ourselves.

These layers continue to build each and every time we have to put up our defenses in order to survive.

A psychospiritual practitioner is a psychotherapist who will meet you as a whole person; body, mind and spirit. Guided by this assistant, you begin the process of psychospiritual therapy. Trusting your process you begin to unravel these layers, dealing with each emotional issue that may arise, in order to get back to your *life*, your pure and wonderful *essence*.

Maybe you, like many people, travel through life stuffing down your true feelings. Food is but one way of accomplishing this stuffing procedure. There are many ways. Do you realize that by stuffing down your true feelings you are pushing away your *true self?*

KEEPING IT SIMPLE

If you were to make a conscious decision to heal your emotions you would no longer feel compelled to do this. Instead, you could gain the understanding that physical well-being is a manifestation of emotional well-being and that physical/emotional well-being when integrated with good spiritual health allows you to trust your process, work through your issues and emerge transformed; unified in body, mind and spirit.

It's all about *choice*. Life is a never-ending realm of decision-making. Your choices determine your reality. Psychospiritual Therapy will reveal how your choices work or don't work in your favour.

Making the choice to believe in yourself and trust your process is where it all starts. And once it begins you discover that you are on a path of personal growth and spiritual development that you will never choose to leave. You will learn to walk the walk that keeps you always true to your *self*, your *higher self* and your *Higher Power*. You will find peace within.

A most important discovery will be that you do, indeed, have choice. You will discover that you can and do make the choices that are right for you. Perhaps on this journey called *life* you have spent far too much time being your own worst enemy.

Through Psychospiritual Therapy you will discover your true *self*. You will meet and learn to love and accept yourself. You can become your own best friend.

***

WHAT IS

A CHAKRA?

The word *chakra* is a Sanskrit word meaning wheel or disk. A wheel-like spinning vortex of energy, a chakra is a point of intersection between various planes or areas of your body. Superimposed on your physical body, you have hundreds of chakras throughout and surrounding you within what is called the *subtle body;* the non-physical psychic body which is made of the more spiritual aspects of yourself.

A chakra is an energy centre and it is the seven major energy centres along the spinal column that have the greatest significance. These seven centres can be thought of as the *master chakras.*

KEEPING IT SIMPLE

Just like flowers, chakras can be open or closed, dying or budding, depending upon the state of well-being and consciousness within.

You will experience the subtle body of energy as thoughts, emotions and feelings. This energy can be measured as electromagnetic force fields that are found within and around you. Kirlian photography has photographed the emanations of the subtle body. These emanations are called the *aura*.

Often made of spindle-like fibers the energy field within the aura appears as a soft glow around the physical body. At your body's core this subtle field appears as spinning disks. These disks are called *chakras*.

These energy centres are gateways between various dimensions. For example, emotional activity connects and plays upon your physical body. This interaction, in turn, plays upon your activities in day to day living and governs your interactions with others.

As an example, take the experience of *fear*. Fear affects your body in certain ways. Perhaps you will feel butterflies in your stomach or maybe your breath becomes short while your voice and hands may shake. These physical characteristics demonstrate a lack of confidence in yourself and may lead others to view you in a negative way, perpetuating your fear.

This fear may not even be grounded in present circumstances but may be a carry-over from childhood which is still buried in the energy centre and ruling your behaviour. To work with the chakras is to heal you of old, restrictive patterns.

To experience what a chakra *feels* like, try the following simple exercise.

KEEPING IT SIMPLE

Extend both arms out in front of you, parallel to the floor, with elbows straight. Turn one hand up and one hand down. Now quickly open and close your hands twenty times or so. Reverse your palms and repeat. Now your hand chakras are open.

To feel them, open your hands and slowly bring your palms together, starting at about two feet apart and moving at a slow rate to a few inches apart. Once your hands are about four inches apart you should be able to feel a subtle ball of energy, like a magnetic field, floating between your palms. If you tune in close, you may even be able to feel the spinning quality. If you hold your hands close to your face you will feel the healing warmth.

A practitioner of *Polarity Therapy*, *Reiki* or *Therapeutic Touch* feels at home with this warm, healing gift.

KEEPING IT SIMPLE

After a few moments the sensation may subside but can be repeated by opening and closing the palms again, as above.

The effect of the energy centres on the physical body is strong for it is believed that the physical body shapes itself around the chakra.

For example, an over-blown solar plexus chakra would manifest in a big, tight belly. A constricted throat chakra results in tight shoulders or a sore throat. A poor connection through the base chakra may show up in skinny legs or bad knees.

Most of us can accept that the way we feel determines the way we act. This, in turn, determines the type of experiences we are likely to have governing the energy that the chakra is likely to draw in toward itself.

KEEPING IT SIMPLE

Conditioning from our parents and culture, physical body shape as well as situations we are born into are important factors and in understanding these patterns you receive valuable insight into your behaviour. If these patterns are beneficial then this self-perpetuation may enhance your personal growth but, if not, then the pattern represents a personal emotional blockage.

In meditation, when working with the chakras, your powers of visualization are utilized. For example, to open your energy centres you may, as Louise L. Hay suggests, choose to visualize a beautiful rosebud transforming into the rose. In order to close your chakras visualize the beautiful rose transforming into a rosebud.

The seven major chakras are associated with seven basic levels of consciousness. However, the seven major energy centres are all inseparably interrelated. A physical, emotional or spiritual block in the functioning of one chakra may affect the activity of the one above or below it.

For example, one may have trouble with his personal power (*solar plexus chakra*) because of a block in communication (*throat chakra*) or vice versa. Or perhaps the real problem may be in your *heart chakra* and only manifest in these other areas because the issue is buried so deep. This kind of situation will be best exemplified by an individual who is unable to feel feelings.

A student can learn to sort out these subtleties and patterns in order to make self-improvement according to his goals.

I will explain this in greater detail as we explore each *chakra* in depth.

***

KEEPING IT SIMPLE

OVERVIEW

OF THE CHAKRA SYSTEM

The names of the seven major chakras are:

Base Chakra

Sacral Chakra

Solar Plexus Chakra

Heart Chakra

Throat Chakra

Brow Chakra

Crown Chakra

 **BASE CHAKRA** is located at the base of the spine. This energy centre is your survival centre, your connection to the earth, your human-ness. When we think of the base chakra we associate it with the colour red.

 **SACRAL CHAKRA** is located below the navel. This energy centre is the centre of all desire; physical, emotional, mental and spiritual. When we think of the sacral chakra we associate it with the colour orange.

 **SOLAR PLEXUS CHAKRA** is located just above the navel and below the breast. This energy centre is the centre of will, determination and perseverance. When we think of the solar plexus chakra we associate it with the colour yellow.

 **HEART CHAKRA** is located between the breast bone and the neck. This energy centre is the centre of unconditional love; love of self and others. A fond reference to the heart chakra is, *"the place where heaven and earth meet."*

This fond reference is used because the base, sacral and solar plexus chakras are all energy centres associated with our human-ness whereas the next three chakras are considered centres of a spiritual nature.

When we think of the heart chakra we associate with it the colours pink or green.

THROAT CHAKRA is located in the area of the throat. This energy centre is the centre of all forms of communication and creativity. When we think of the throat chakra we associate with it the colour blue.

BROW CHAKRA is located in the centre of the forehead. This energy centre is the centre of our understanding. When we think of the brow chakra we associate with it the colour indigo.

CROWN CHAKRA is located in the top centre of the head. This energy centre is the connection to your higher self and to your Higher Power. When we think of the crown chakra we associate with it the colour purple or white.

In the following chapters I will discuss each major chakra in greater depth.

***

BASE CHAKRA

Base Chakra

The base chakra is located at the base of the spine. Its element is the earth and this energy centre represents your connection to the earth. This is the centre of your groundedness, your human-ness. The physical body parts associated with the base chakra are the low back, the legs, feet and intestines.

KEEPING IT SIMPLE

The colour associated with the base chakra is red; the colour of the life force. If you feel tired, wear a red sweater, a red scarf or anything that is red and you will feel energized.

When you resist the life force or, in other words, have difficulty going with the flow of life, the result is often anger. Anger is also symbolized by the colour red, for example, *"I saw red when ……."*

If you think of the base chakra as the base of a tree then it is easy to understand why this energy centre is associated with your connection to the earth, in fact, your very survival. When you feel safe and secure the energy in your base chakra is free to flow.

There are all kinds of security; for example, emotional, physical, financial, mental or spiritual security.

KEEPING IT SIMPLE

If you are feeling insecure in any or all of these areas of life it is quite likely that your base chakra will be blocked and you will experience pain.

It is in this centre that the battle of scarcity versus abundance is waged. If you are fearful and anxious about providing the basic necessities for this human experience called life, working with the base chakra will enable you to transform this fear and anxiety into a confidence and a knowing that your needs will be met.

There are many emotional issues you may experience that impact the base chakra. If these emotional issues are worked through and healed it is possible to avoid the physical manifestation of, for example, low back pain; leg, knee or foot injuries; constipation or diarrhea.

KEEPING IT SIMPLE

If the emotional issues have not been worked through and you are currently experiencing the manifestation of these physical ailments, it is possible, by working with the base chakra, to find the emotional source of the physical ailment. You can experience emotional healing and eliminate the need for the physical injury or illness.

Below is a list containing some examples of emotional issues associated with the base chakra.

Fear of Abandonment

Fear of Engulfment

Control Issues

Insecurity Issues

Fearfulness

Powerlessness

Fear of Change

KEEPING IT SIMPLE

Now I will focus in more depth on each of these emotional issues.

Fear of Abandonment

Perhaps as a child you experienced what you perceived to be abandonment. Perhaps your care-givers just were not there for you or perhaps they were there but you didn't feel that they were there for you in the way that you needed. This feeling of abandonment created extreme fright within you. Yet, somehow, you learned to cope and, yes, you did survive.

However you have noticed that in adult relationships you fear that the relationship will not last. You fear that your partner will leave you. Sometimes your fear of abandonment is so great that you will end the relationship yourself to avoid the possibility of being left by another.

Sometimes your fear of abandonment is so great that you will not allow yourself to enter into a relationship. Instead you will travel through life as a *loner* who is always on the outside looking in. You don't enjoy this role but, for you, it feels safer somehow than risking further abandonment.

Fear of abandonment results in a blocked base chakra. These emotional wounds, if left undetected and untreated, will manifest in physical pain and suffering. Perhaps you will injure your knee rather than go forward in a relationship or perhaps you will suffer from extreme lower back pain.

Fear of Engulfment:

This fear is the opposite side of the coin called Fear of Abandonment. These two fears are often demonstrated in an individual who seems to say to his partner, *"Come here. No, I don't want you here. Go away and leave me alone. No, don't go. I need you. Come here. No, I don't want you here."* This pattern of behaviour can go on in a painful, repetitive cycle until the emotional wounds of fear of abandonment/engulfment are recognized, honoured and transformed.

Control Issues:

is a subtle distinction between the terms *in control of yourself* and being *self-controlled.*

An individual who is self-controlled is one who knows who he is; one who presents who he is feeling comfortable in any situation. This person does not have to think about trying to control himself or others. He simply is self-controlled.

On the other hand a person who feels *in control of self* is an individual who feels the need to be in control.

Let's make this close and personal.

If you feel a need to be in control, whether you are aware of it or not, you are demonstrating to yourself that you are not in control of self. You would not feel a need to be something that you already know you are.

KEEPING IT SIMPLE

Just as an honest person does not need to try to be honest, a self-controlled individual does not need to try to be in control of self.

But if you do feel a need to be in control then, no doubt, you have experienced that you easily lose control of yourself when presented with serious life challenges. This loss of control may manifest in one of many emotional ways.

>For example, just to name a few:
>
>*Tears*
>
>*Sadness*
>
>*Depression*
>
>*Rigidity*
>
>*Outward Anger*
>
>*Addiction*
>
>*Rage*
>
>*Violence*

KEEPING IT SIMPLE

Speaking in general, a person who is self-controlled lives with the awareness that he has no control over another's actions, thoughts or being. Further, a self-controlled person has no desire to control another.

On the other hand, a person who feels a need to be in control of himself will probably also feel a need to control the thoughts and actions of others who play a role in his life experience.

Consider it this way: If you feel the need to control people, situations, and events in your world the odds are you feel out of control yourself. You may think that if you can control everyone and everything around you then you will feel in control of yourself. Of course, it never works. This is a futile exercise with an impossible goal.

By working with the base chakra and further addressing these control issues in psychospiritual therapy you can discover what early events in your life created these original control issues. With this new awareness your control issues can be worked through with success.

Trying to control self can be transformed into self-control.

Meditation is one wonderful tool to assist in bringing unconscious control issues into consciousness in order that the issues can be recognized, honoured and dealt with in a safe environment.

Insecurity Issues:

Insecurity is another issue associated with the base chakra. There are many forms in which insecurity may manifest in your life experience. The insecurity may be physical or financial, for example.

However, all insecurity is an emotional experience with a solid foundation in fear. The outward manifestation of insecurity may be physical or financial however, by focusing attention on the base chakra in meditation and by working with the base chakra in psychospiritual therapy; you can further address these fears. They are probably rooted in childhood and you can discover that the yearned for security can be provided by yourself, to yourself.

Fearfulness:

Fearfulness is another issue associated with the base chakra. Fear is an emotion which is both powerful and useful. Fear will alert you to real danger and will prompt you to take action in order to guarantee personal safety,

However, fearfulness, as an emotional issue with the power to block the base chakra, is something entirely different.

If you experience fearfulness you are often and possibly always fearful. Did you know that fear is the opposite of love?

Did you know that it is possible, through meditation, to recognize and own your fearfulness?

And it is possible, through psychospiritual therapy, to work through these issues of fearfulness and to discover the light of love within. Shining the light of love on those events in your life experience that triggered the fear, it is possible to transform this powerful emotion called fear into a more powerful one called love.

Powerlessness:

Another emotional issue associated with the base chakra is powerlessness. A definition of powerlessness might be *fearfulness in the extreme,*

The majority of us experience a feeling of powerlessness in early childhood in relation to our parents, teachers and other authority figures. This subtle sense of powerlessness is natural given that as a small child you are dependent upon others to care for your basic needs. When these needs were met in childhood you developed trust in others. And by learning to trust significant others you were encouraged to learn to trust in yourself. As you grew older you matured and began to experience your own power.

When your needs were not met by those upon whom you were dependent in childhood this feeling of powerlessness grew as you did and some of you have taken this sense of powerlessness into adulthood.

An individual who had this negative type of childhood experience lacks self-trust. If this was the case in your life you will often feel inadequate and, yes, powerless to act in your own best interest and that of others. You may remain dependent upon others to meet your needs yet you will often continue to choose to have others in your life who are unable or unwilling to meet your needs.

A person who experiences powerlessness is often a victim of the whims and choices of others. If this is the case for you then you may often feel unhappy. You may feel there is nothing you can do to change your life situation.

KEEPING IT SIMPLE

In an extreme situation an individual can be literally paralyzed by these overwhelming feelings of powerlessness.

Focusing on the base chakra in meditation may assist you in recognizing and honouring your feelings of powerlessness. Again another crossroads in life is reached. Should you find the faith in yourself, even though it be *as tiny as a mustard seed*, to make a conscious choice in seeking psychospiritual therapy you will, in this process, find the courage to seek out, discover and honour your own choices. Through transformational counseling and daily meditation you can change from one who feels powerless to one who is empowered.

Fear of Change:

This is another emotional issue associated with the base chakra. We truly live in a world that is constantly changing.

If you hang onto the belief system that *I've always done it this way and this is the way I am going to continue* or *I've always felt this way and this is the way I will always feel* then you will find that you are emotionally *stuck*.

By focusing on the base chakra in meditation you can acknowledge your fear of change, honour it and own it. Should you choose to transform this fear into a loving, open, secure sense of self you will find yourself on a path of personal growth. You will also find that you are capable of being a participant in the adventure of life; one that is both satisfying and rewarding.

Summing up the base chakra:

In quick summary some of the emotional issues of the base chakra include fear of abandonment/engulfment; control issues; feelings of insecurity; fearfulness and in the extreme, powerlessness and a fear of change.

Meditation will allow you to get in touch with your inner self; the place where all these issues are sourced. Through meditation you will be able to shine the light on these dark, shadowy aspects of yourself. Once owned you become aware that you, indeed, have choice.

You can choose to live your life repressing/expressing these shadow parts of yourself OR through psychospiritual therapy you can choose to work through these issues and experience the transformational process which leads to a more peaceful, fulfilling life experience.

KEEPING IT SIMPLE

The base chakra is associated with your sense of safety, security and survival. This energy centre is located at the base of the spine. It is your connection to the earth and can be likened to the roots of a tree. It's an old cliché but we are reminded that *the apple does not fall far from the tree.*

If the roots are unhealthy the tree will not flourish and bear nourishing, healthy fruit. Likewise, if your base chakra is emotionally blocked, you will manifest an unhappy, unhealthy life experience ruled by fear.

A *Meditation for the Base Chakra follows.*

***

MEDITATION

FOR BASE CHAKRA

Relax as you sit with your hands on your knees, palms upward to receive. Close your eyes. Breathe deeply. Allow the cares and worries of your day to evaporate as though they had never existed. You are here; present in the moment. Allow your body and your mind to be still.

Imagine a portal opening above you in the centre of the room. See streams of white light (prana) pouring through this portal. Allow this divine, creative, healing light to enfold you in its warmth.

Invite the light to enter your body beginning at your feet. Feel the light travel up through your legs to your base chakra located at the base of your spine. Allow your focus to centre on your base chakra.

KEEPING IT SIMPLE

This energy centre is associated with survival and its element is earth. Its colour is red.

Open your base chakra. See it open, receptive. Release the brilliant red. See this red light merge with the white light until your base chakra is filled with white and red; blending separating, merging together.

Your base chakra is open and receptive. Allow the healing white light to fill your base chakra as you affirm your personal power with confidence and love. Affirm: *I am part of all that is. I am grounded in the knowledge that I am never alone. As I travel along my path I know that my needs are met. I visualize a world of plenty, prosperity and peace and I know that what I can visualize I can actualize.*

My Higher Power protects me. My higher self instructs me. Within myself I discover inner strength and courage that allows me to feel my connection to the earth on which I stand. I am safe. I am peaceful. I am healthy and prosperous.

I ask and my questions are answered. I am open to receive and my needs are met. I express my personal power. What my mind can conceive and believe I can achieve.

I believe in the creative power within me. I believe in my ability to change. I am centred in a creative flow of prosperity in possession of my desired goals. I say yes to prosperity, good health and healthy relationships. I express my personal power with confidence and love. I am part of all that is. I am never alone.

Now as you see the portal above you closing, close and seal your base chakra with love.

Prepare yourself to return to the room. Feel your feet grounded and solid upon the floor. Send

KEEPING IT SIMPLE

grounding rods deep within the earth and know that you are firmly anchored and centred.

When you feel ready, open your eyes.

***

SACRAL CHAKRA

Sacral Chakra

Located in the lower abdomen one to two inches below the navel is the Sacral Chakra which is sometimes called the Sexual Chakra. The Sacral Chakra is known as *the seat of desire; physical, emotional and spiritual.*

KEEPING IT SIMPLE

This energy centre controls your sexuality, desires, passions and feelings. This is where you balance your male/female energies.

Here, you are able to feel and experience both painful and negative emotions. This chakra is associated with your ability to achieve intimacy with yourself and with others.

Body image is such a big issue for many people, especially women, today. It is in this chakra that your sense of your own body image is centred and it can be associated with sexual shame or body shame which was most often established in early childhood.

I am sure you have heard the old saying, *"Sticks and stones may break my bones but words can never hurt me."*

There is truth in this old adage for those who have a strong sense of self. Critical, condemning words will not be hurtful. They will simply be like drops of water rolling off a duck's back.

However, in the vulnerability of childhood, up until the age of reason which is approximately seven or eight years of age in the *average* child, critical words can be like sharp knives cutting into the promise of a stable, well-adjusted adult.

Parents, teachers, authority figures in a young child's life are not always aware of the damage they are doing when they criticize the *child* instead of the *child's behaviour.* As an example, when a child hears the words, *"You are stupid"* or *"You are an ugly child"* these insults will be absorbed like a sponge and the child will feel stupid and ugly.

By using such terms and attacking the child's very being; incredible damage is done to the child's sense of self. Too often these feelings of low self-esteem are carried into adulthood accompanied by issues around body image.

And, of course, there are emotional issues associated with a blocked sacral chakra.

It is here that we discover our ability for *melodrama*. There are those of us who do not need to turn on the T.V. to watch a soap opera. We merely need to observe our own lives and recognize the role we are playing in the drama, the comedy, the thriller or the tragedy.

If you have this ability and if you carried this ability to the extreme you would discover that you cannot go from one day to the next without a crisis. An apt, if unflattering, term for anyone with this issue could be *Crisis Junkie*. In the extreme your life will be filled with crisis after crisis. And, most often, you will be unaware that you are using these crises as a method of avoiding looking within and discovering who you really are.

Below I will make a list of the many emotional issues associated with the sacral chakra.

NUMBING OUT:

When you cannot allow yourself to feel feelings, *numbing out* takes place. It's a defense mechanism which protects you from feeling emotional pain. It is a two-sided coin, however, because your success in numbing out also prevents you from feeling emotional joy or happiness. You may become robotic in nature, living by rote, following safe routines and avoiding all possibility of pain. Unfortunately you are also successfully blocking yourself from personal freedom and growth to become a healthy, whole individual.

REPRESSING/DENYING FEELINGS:

Imagine if you will, a bucket of water and visualize a rubber ball floating atop the water. Now imagine placing your hand on the ball, forcing it to the bottom of the bucket, not allowing it to surface. Imagine how tired your arm will become after a little time passes. Imagine how absolutely useless your arm will become if it is always held in this position holding the ball at the bottom of the water-filled bucket.

If you repress feelings and, in the extreme, if you deny your feelings, you are, in effect, tiring and, perhaps both emotionally and physically, exhausting yourself in your efforts to keep your feelings repressed. Just imagine how numb you will feel if you continue on this path. Imagine how useless your life could become.

The sacral chakra is the seat of all desire. By denying your desires and their accompanying feelings, this energy centre will become blocked. And, when this happens, your potential for owning, feeling and expressing feelings is stymied and stuck.

If you were to focus on the sacral energy centre in meditation it would become possible for you to recognize this repression and denial within you. When you are able to bring this recognition into your awareness it will become possible to make a decision for change.

And through psychospiritual therapy you will be able to learn how to feel feelings safely; how to understand the origin of the emotional shut-down and to take steps toward a more full and satisfying life experience.

FEAR OF INTIMACY

Another emotional issue associated with the sacral chakra is fear of intimacy. If you did not achieve a close, loving relationship with a caretaking adult in early childhood then it is likely that you will have difficulty achieving a close, loving relationship with yourself.

And if you have not achieved an intimate relationship with yourself, you will find it impossible to achieve this desired intimacy with another.

It is easier to understand how the fear of intimacy takes root if you are able to keep in mind that *fear* and *love* are opposite sides of the same coin. Consider this: If you are unable to find love within for yourself how can you share love with others?

By the same token, if you are afraid to know who you are and if you have repressed or denied your feelings; possibly numbed out, then you will not achieve an intimate relationship with yourself. And taking it one step further, if you are unable to achieve intimacy with yourself, how can you be intimate with another?

Please keep in mind that when I talk about intimacy I am speaking of intimacy on all levels: physical, sexual, mental, emotional and spiritual.

Fear of intimacy can be recognized during meditation which is focused on the sacral chakra. And, as with all issues, if this fear is recognized, honoured and owned, then it is possible through psychospiritual therapy to discover the origin of this fear and to work through the emotional pain associated with this issue in a safe environment.

It is possible and it is never too late to develop an intimate relationship with self. Once this is achieved it is possible to develop intimate relationships with others.

FEAR OF REJECTION

Like all fears, the fear of rejection has the potential to manifest in reality. And this fear is another emotional issue that can be associated with the sacral chakra which is the seat of desire.

Now, just to explain, imagine you have the desire to be hired in a new position. Your yearning is strong but your fear of rejection, introduced to you in early childhood, is even stronger than your desire. *What will you do?*

Perhaps you will cancel your job interview appointment, assuming you had the courage to make one.

Or if you find the courage to attend the job interview you take your fear of rejection along with you. And, of course, this negative energy will be picked up by the person conducting the interview and your fear of rejection will once more be affirmed.

You were afraid you would be rejected and, lo and behold, your services were rejected; a self-fulfilling prophecy.

By getting in touch with your inner self during a meditation focused on the sacral chakra you will allow yourself to get in touch with your fear of rejection. This recognition, if accepted, acknowledged and owned, will soon open new doors for you.

Through psychospiritual therapy you can place your focus on this and other emotional issues of the sacral chakra. You can begin the transformational process that will lead to self-acceptance. Once you learn to accept yourself you will no longer reject yourself. And once you are able to stop rejecting yourself you will soon lose the fear of rejection.

Instead you will enjoy the adventure of life, meeting new experiences and challenges with love, confidence and good self-esteem.

We have discussed some of the emotional issues associated with the sacral chakra including numbing out, repressing/denying feelings, fear of intimacy and fear of rejection.

Sometimes these issues are accompanied by addictions to sex, love, crisis or even alcohol and drugs. And sometimes these very same issues are unaccompanied by these addictions yet the individual will find himself being an enabler to another who has one or another or perhaps all of the above addictions.

If you have these emotional issues and if you allow yourself to be in a relationship at all, the odds are you will find yourself in a co-dependent relationship. Your role will be either that of addict or enabler. Both roles are, of course, opposite sides of the same coin because in this type of unhealthy relationship you can't have one without the other.

A meditation for the Sacral (sexual) Chakra follows.

***

MEDITATION

FOR SACRAL (SEXUAL) CHAKRA

Relax as you sit with your hands on your knees, palms upward to receive. Close your eyes. Breathe deeply. Allow the cares and worries of your day to evaporate as though they had never existed. You are here, present in the moment. Allow your body and your mind to be still.

Imagine a portal above you in the centre of the room. See streams of white light pouring through this portal. Allow this divine creative, healing light to enfold you in its warmth.

Invite the light to enter your body beginning at your feet. Feel it travel up through your legs, through your base chakra to your sacral chakra located in your lower abdomen. Allow your focus to centre on your sacral chakra which is associated with sexual desire, passion and feelings; the balancing of your male and female energies; your ability to be intimate with yourself and others. Its element is water and its colour is orange.

Open your sacral chakra. Release the brilliant orange. See this orange light merge with the white light. Your sacral chakra is filled now with white and orange, blending, separating and merging together.

As you allow the healing white light to fill your sacral chakra you affirm your personal power with confidence and love. Allow yourself to receive the following affirmations;

I am open to know myself. I am open to intimacy with myself. I visualize the people with whom I feel most close and I see myself sharing relationship with them in an open, caring and truthful manner. I allow myself to experience feelings, both hot and cold, that until now have possibly been repressed by fear of rejection or fear of intimacy.

I am confident, loving, and open to express myself freely with caring and compassion.

I accept my body from the tip of my toes to the top of my head. I am good to my body, giving it the rest, the exercise, the healthy food it desires. I feel good about myself and these feelings of good are expressed through my body, my actions, and my walk along my path.

I no longer desire crisis in my life. I seek peace and a balance of my male and female energies. I am in touch with who I am and I like who I am. I choose what I do and I will not be under the power and influence of sex, love, crisis, and alcohol or drug addiction.

KEEPING IT SIMPLE

In the white light I know that awareness plus acceptance plus action will equal transformational change within me.

I am open to receive and I say yes to my sexuality. I say yes to my feelings, both warm and cool. I say yes to my body and I affirm my ability and desire to care for myself in a healthy way. I express my personal power with confidence and love.

Now see the portal above you closing. Close and seal your sacral chakra with love.

Prepare yourself to return to the room. Feel your feet grounded and solid on the floor. Send grounding rods deep within the earth ensuring your sense of centredness and balance in your being.

When you feel ready, open your eyes.

***

KEEPING IT SIMPLE

SOLAR PLEXUS CHAKRA

Solar Plexus Chakra

Located in the middle of your abdomen just above the navel is your solar plexus chakra. It is described as *the seat of personal power*. Its colour is yellow, the colour of the sun. When you are empowered you shine like the sun. When you feel powerless you could be called *yellow*. The element of the solar plexus energy centre is fire. Perhaps you are not surprised to learn that the solar plexus is the storage tank for your repressed anger; hence the term *fire down below*.

When anger is simmering within you this simmering can be likened to the yellow embers of a fire. It is anyone's guess when the embers will die out or burst into flame.

Here in the solar plexus chakra you discover your personal power and your will to act upon desire. It is also in this energy centre that your boundary setting abilities are situate and this is where you will discover your true essence or identity.

If you have no strong emotional boundaries in place you will often feel powerless. You will wonder why people are *always walking all over you.*

The polarity of this situation may be that you are an angry, powerful person who makes the wrong use of your power. You may find yourself lashing out at others; dominating and alienating those around you.

Neither of these polarities, powerlessness nor powerfulness, are desirable attributes. The middle road of *personal empowerment* is key to emotional health. Once you have worked through your rage and anger issues you will feel centred, well-balanced and grounded. You will feel empowered to make healthy choices for your life.

There are many emotional issues which have a negative impact in regard to the solar plexus chakra. If you are able to recognize, accept and honour these issues in your meditation you will soon discover it is possible to take the necessary steps, with the help of psychospiritual therapy, to work through and heal these wounds.

In this way you can prevent the physical manifestation of ailments such as stomach ulcers for example.

However if these issues have already resulted in physical illness it is possible, through psychospiritual therapy, to discover the original emotional source of the illness. Once you have been able to do this you can work through the issues and begin to walk the path of physical and emotional wellness.

Addictions associated with the solar plexus chakra include power, work and money.

It is not surprising to learn that so-called *workaholics*; people who hide from themselves in their work, are usually of an underweight to medium physical build. A workaholic may appear to be in good physical health but looks can be deceiving. Workaholics often suffer with stomach ulcers.

KEEPING IT SIMPLE

If you are burying, repressing or denying feelings of anger you will often have the physical appearance of one with a bulging stomach. You may or may not be overweight in other parts of your body but it is definite that the solar plexus area of your body will be swollen with anger that is hidden by fat.

In my view, the so-called *jolly fat person* is an individual out of touch with the repressed anger and hostility buried within.

If this person is you, then I hope you will consider meeting with a good therapist who will assist you in dealing with the triggering effect of these long-buried emotions as they emerge.

Below is a list of the many emotional issues associated with the Solar Plexus Chakra.

Powermonger versus Victim

Control over Others

Lack of Boundaries

Unable to Stand up for Self

Nice People

People Pleaser

And now I will go into more depth on each of the issues.

POWERMONGER versus VICTIM:

These two issues are polarities or, to use a more familiar term, they are opposite sides of the same coin.

Although sometimes not clearly evident, if you are an individual assuming the role of *victim* in life, you can be quite powerful in your control over others. Also, again not always clearly evident, if you are a person who appears to be a *Powermonger* it is probable that in your early childhood experience you were a *victim*. As such you continue to victimize yourself and others by your wrong use of power.

I will talk first about the *powermonger*. You may be wondering what a powermonger is. I think a good definition might be that *a powermonger is an unhappy individual who, in his attempt to feel in control, finds it necessary to exert control over others.*

KEEPING IT SIMPLE

This kind of power mongering can be demonstrated in subtle ways in the home or work place or even behind the wheel of a car. A powermonger is out of touch with his feelings and will take little responsibility for those things in life that are not going well. Instead he will blame everyone around him for everything that is not to his satisfaction.

In the workplace the powermonger is the boss who never listens to the thoughts or idea of his employees but operates always from the top down.

Behind the wheel of a car, this person is a menace to society; never giving way, cursing other drivers and ignoring speed laws.

A powermonger takes pleasure in putting other people down and his own sense of importance is dependent upon his belief that others are less important, less valid and less powerful.

More simply put, a powermonger is a *bully*.

The bully is scared to death inside but is not close enough to his true self to be aware of his fear. As a result he goes through life projecting his fears in a bullying, domineering manner onto others who have the misfortune of sharing the path of life with him.

And this takes us to the other side of the coin. The people who share life with a powermonger are called *victims*. And what is a victim? One definition might be that a victim is one who, like the bully, is not in touch with his own feelings. The victim is also scared. As a consequence, when the powermonger bellows, the victim cowers.

Both individuals utilize power in an unhealthy way. Neither one is empowered. Neither are happy people.

KEEPING IT SIMPLE

Until now I have been talking about this issue with adults in mind. I feel it is necessary to make a distinction when talking about children.

Yes, there are many children who, through parental example, have learned to become bullies. These children are, in fact, victims.

However there are many children who are victimized by parents, caretakers and other authority figures and these children are truly the *innocent victims* in our society. They deserve and need your love, compassion and help as do all children.

It is unfortunate, indeed, that these children who are victimized through emotional, verbal, physical, and even sexual abuse, if not rescued, loved and cared for in a healthy way, will grow into adults who continue the cycle of victimization.

KEEPING IT SIMPLE

If intervention does not take place, a child who is abused will grow into an adult who continues to be abused or, conversely, one who abuses others. This is because the emotional issues of powermonger and victim are opposite sides of the same coin.

There are more subtle feelings of victimization in people who use the *victim role* as a way of wielding power. To give you an example of this, consider an individual who is a victim in life; one who cannot find or hold a job; one who cannot take responsible action to meet his own needs. This so-called *victim* personality, in a covert way, controls the actions and behaviours of those in his life. He is the *poor me* who can't seem to do anything right or the one who is consistently dependent upon others.

If not conscious of the power the victim is capable of wielding, her partner in life will discover that he is forever being *sucked in* to a situation where everything needs to be his decision, his responsibility and his burden to bear.

The victim's partner, if not careful, becomes *a victim of the victim.*

It is usual for powermongers to seek out victims in relationship. And it is also usual for victims to subconsciously seek out powermongers.

One powermonger will rarely seek out another but sometimes one victim will seek out another victim. Perhaps this is where the cliché, *misery loves company,* originates.

Meditation will enable the powermonger/victim to gain some recognition of these emotional issues which are blocking the solar plexus chakra. Help is, indeed, available for these individuals through psychospiritual therapy.

KEEPING IT SIMPLE

If these issues are yours, rest assured it is possible to discover the origin of the emotional wounds. And it is possible to work through the pain in a safe way and to begin to find the middle ground; the balance which is *empowerment.*

CONTROL OVER OTHERS

The need to have control over others is another emotional issue associated with the Solar Plexus Chakra. I have already talked about this when discussing the powermonger/victim issues where control over others is taken to the extreme and where this control is an obvious abuse of power.

A less obvious emotional issue is *control over others*. For example, there are areas in life where healthy control over others is called for. The best example of this is when parenting children. If a child is playing on the road, it is hoped that a parent will exert his control over the child and bring him back onto the safety of the sidewalk or into the backyard.

Healthy, loving, disciplining of children is a form of control over others which is necessary to guarantee the physical and emotional safety and well-being of the child.

But the emotional issue of control over others is often demonstrated by individuals who feel a need to control their environment. Because they lack self-control they are always endeavoring to be in control of themselves as well as in control of the feelings and actions of others. Speaking in general terms, they are tense individuals. They are rigid in their thinking and behaviour. This is the person who will keep his hands on the household purse and bank account. Money is recognized as power and by controlling the spending of others they strive to maintain some semblance of control. This is the person who sets rules and expects others to abide by them. This is the person who has his thumb down on the heads of all with whom he shares life's path. She will often feel tight as a drum; taut as an elastic band being stretched to its limits; rigid as a piece of steel. And because he is out of touch with his true, inner self he is, indeed, a difficult person with whom to live.

LACK OF BOUNDARIES

Another emotional issue associated with the Solar Plexus Chakra is a lack of emotional and, consequently, physical boundaries.

Your lack of boundaries will be demonstrated in many ways. ; For example, you will often not recognize the difference between *your stuff* and *my stuff* whether that *stuff* is material or emotional.

If this is one of your issues you will probably borrow without asking and you will see nothing wrong when another does the same to you. You will possibly read your partner's emails. You may even go so far as to answer your partner's emails. You will, no doubt, allow another to butt into your affairs and have no inner sense of privacy. Neither will you respect the emotional privacy of another.

KEEPING IT SIMPLE

If this is one of your issues, confess, you are a *gossip*. You are one who spreads tales about others with no thought of consequence. You soak up like a sponge the problems and troubles of others and, in this way, you do not take the time to do any inner work or to take a look at your own state of affairs.

It is unfortunate but there are many homes in which no boundaries exist; where doors are never closed, not even bathroom doors. There are homes in which a private diary may be read aloud to all family members in the living room.

Living in a home with a lack of boundaries will promote a lack of self-respect and, of course, if you lack self-respect there is small hope you will respect the needs and desires of others.

If you know that you lack boundaries you can, through meditation on the Solar Plexus Chakra and through psychospiritual therapy, learn how to set healthy boundaries, both physical and emotional. Setting and maintaining healthy boundaries is essential to emotional wellness.

Having talked a little about the emotional issue of *lack of boundaries* leads me to the next emotional issue associated with the Solar Plexus Chakra which is the *inability to stand up for self.*

UNABLE TO STAND UP FOR SELF

When you fail to set healthy physical and emotional boundaries it is safe to say you will lack assertiveness.

You will recognize the non-assertive individual when you meet him. He is the one who is unable to stand up for himself. She is the one whose mechanic cheats her but she pays with a smile. He feels doomed to lose arguments and he gives way even when he knows he is right. She tenses up when she's in a difficult situation, knowing she should be assertive but afraid to try. When attacked by others, he won't know how to deal with the situation. He is terrified of confrontation of any kind and will go to any and all lengths to avoid it. He will hope for peace at any price.

She has a low opinion of herself and is not surprised when people walk all over her demonstrating that they also have a low opinion of her. An individual who is unable to stand up for himself is a fearful person who rarely, if ever, voices opinions or makes decisions.

This is the spouse who aggravates his partner with his monotonous, meaningless, ineffective, *Yes, dear* and *Well, I suppose so.* Keep in mind, an individual who is unable to stand up for himself would be an unlikely candidate for a position of standing up for another.

He may be described as a mild-mannered milquetoast who wouldn't hurt a fly. But is it true that he is not hurting anyone? I don't think so. And the person he is hurting the most is himself.

NICE PEOPLE

You may be wondering how *nice person* can be the name of a negative emotional issue. Generally speaking a well-balanced, emotionally healthy individual is one who is able to feel and express in a healthy way all of his wide-ranging feelings. Perhaps sometimes he is nice but sometimes he is not. It is expected that a healthy human being has access to and free, healthy expression of an extremely wide range of emotions.

There are those among us who feel the need to appear as always a *nice person*. If this is you then you may be described as being nice, sweet, charming, friendly, always nice, nice and nice. If this describes you then you will not know how to deal with anyone who is not nice. You will see the world through rose-coloured glasses and strive to keep the world at a distance. You can be so entrenched in *niceness* that when anything at all gets out of kilter you will know it is not your fault. How could it be? You are always so *nice*. You will keep your cool when all around you others are losing it. You will walk away and leave the room when unpleasantness occurs.

You don't want to hear about any so-called not nice feelings in another; for example, anger, sadness or fear. It is certain you will never admit that you ever feel these feelings.

The truth is you probably don't. You are afraid of these feelings and strive to keep them buried within. You will always have a kind word to say as long as there are no difficult issues with which to deal.

This so-called *nice person* will look for the nearest *bitch* to take care of it for him.

KEEPING IT SIMPLE

Nice people avoid confrontation. And nice people truly believe that they are always nice. No one could ever convince them otherwise.

But it is rare, indeed, that this person will find the courage to go within to discover what is often evident to others about them and that is the *motivation* behind all this *niceness*.

These people wear their niceness like a suit of armor to keep all unpleasantness away.

These nice people always ensure that they have someone in their lives to take care of those things that are not so nice. The individual who coined the phrase, *Beware the nice guy!* is offering timely advice.

Meditation with the focus on the Solar Plexus Chakra will give the *nice* practitioner an opportunity to look within and to observe the rigidity of this so-called niceness.

KEEPING IT SIMPLE

If you feel this issue applies to you then, if you choose, it is possible to get in touch with deeper feelings and emotions through psychospiritual therapy. You can discover the potential to transform into a *real person* with a wide range of emotions available for you to use in the expression of your true essence, your true identity. You can begin to understand that *it is not always nice to be nice.*

PEOPLE PLEASER

A people pleaser is somewhat similar to a *nice* person.

If you are a people pleaser, you will go out of your way to please and pacify others. You will be kept busy trying to please and meet the needs of others. As a consequence you will often neglect your own needs.

A people pleaser is not a happy person. She is always striving for acceptance, to be liked and to be wanted.

If this is you, then rest assured that through quiet meditation you can become acquainted with this emotional issue within. Through psychospiritual therapy, if you so choose, you can learn self-acceptance and self-love.

KEEPING IT SIMPLE

You can learn that pleasing others can be a conscious choice and that it does not have to be a need that is always driving you further away from who you truly can be.

By learning to please yourself, you will learn that others are capable of doing the same. You can learn that pleasing yourself can be very pleasing to those who love you. And you can learn that sometimes it is desirable to please others but not at the expense of self. To *please and love thy neighbour as ye please and love yourself* is the goal.

A meditation for the Solar Plexus Chakra follows.

***

MEDITATION

FOR THE SOLAR PLEXUS CHAKRA

Relax as you sit with your hands on your knees, palms upward to receive. Close your eyes. Breathe deeply. Allow the cares and the worries of your day to evaporate as though they had never existed. You are here; present in the moment. Allow your body and your mind to be still.

Be still, my mind.

Imagine a portal opening above you in the centre of the room. See streams of white light pouring through this portal. Allow this divine, creative, healing light to enfold you in its warmth.

Invite the light to enter your body beginning at your feet. Feel the light travel up through your legs, through your base chakra, your sacral chakra to your solar plexus chakra located in the middle of your abdomen just above the navel. Allow your focus to remain on this energy centre which is associated with personal power and identity; the power of will and your mental abilities. The solar plexus chakra is also associated with boundaries and your ability to assert yourself.

Open your solar plexus chakra. Release the brilliant yellow. See this yellow light merge with the white light until the chakra is filled with white and yellow; blending, separating and merging together.

As you allow the healing, white light to fill your solar plexus chakra you affirm your personal power with confidence and love. And you accept as your own the following affirmations.

I assert myself in my world in a peaceful way. I am strong within myself and although it feels good to find that others may agree with my choices, I no longer seek or need the approval of others. I am capable of making good choices for myself. My judgment is sound. I approve of me. I am at peace within.

I acknowledge the anger I have repressed and I am able to find safe, healthy ways to express this anger. I am finding safe, healthy ways to express current day anger. Old rage no longer controls me.

I enjoy my work but I ensure that I take the time to rest, relax and allow other activities and other people into my world. My work no longer controls me. I know that my needs, be they emotional, spiritual or material, are balanced in a healthy way.

I am not a powermonger. I am not a victim.

I feel empowered and I can say this is me *and* this is not me. *In this way I make my choices.*

KEEPING IT SIMPLE

I recognize that each individual soul that I meet along my path is whole and complete as I am whole and complete. I establish healthy boundaries and ensure that enmeshment is a thing of the past.

In the white light I know that awareness plus acceptance plus action will equal transformational change within me.

I am open to receive and I say yes to self-assertiveness. I say yes to good anger management. I say yes to personal empowerment. I express my personal power with humility, confidence and love.

Now see the portal above you closing. Close and seal your solar plexus chakra with love. Prepare yourself to return to the room. Feel your feet grounded solid on the floor.

KEEPING IT SIMPLE

Send grounding rods deep within the earth to ensure your sense of centredness and balance within your being.

When you feel ready, open your eyes.

***

HEART CHAKRA

Heart Chakra

The Heart Chakra is located in the upper chest in the area of your heart. Its colours are pink or green. Pink seems to be the colour traditionally chosen to celebrate matters of the heart as we might do on St. Valentine's Day, for example. However green is the colour of life and one who loves life will find green an appropriate colour to symbolize the heart chakra.

KEEPING IT SIMPLE

Up until now I have talked a little about the base chakra, the sacral chakra and the solar plexus chakra. Each of these energy centres is associated with your human-ness; those parts of you that are connected to the earth and the human experience.

The heart chakra is the centre of your being and it is from this centre that the flow of energy commences its spiral down to the Solar Plexus Chakra, up to the Throat Chakra, down to the Sacral Chakra, up to the Brow Chakra, down to the Base Chakra and up to the Crown Chakra.

The throat, brow and crown chakras are considered to be of the spirit; of heaven.

For this reason and with fondness, the Heart Chakra is called *the place where heaven and earth meet.*

KEEPING IT SIMPLE

The Heart Chakra has been called that perfect place where heaven and earth meet and in so doing, when we make this connection, we are able to transform and integrate our dual nature; that of the body and of the mind and spirit. This energy centre is the home of unconditional love with no agenda. It is from here that we are able to feel, experience and express our love for self and for others.

From this chakra we give and we receive.

It is the home of self-love; loving our strengths but also loving and respecting our limitations. The inner child's first choice of residence is within the heart chakra.

It is from this place that you express grief. Whether the loss is that of a loved one, a job, one's childhood, one's sense of self or one's motivation to grow; grieving your losses is a spiritual process that encompasses all human emotions. Through your heart chakra you experience shame, healing and the essence of unconditional love.

There are many emotional issues associated with the Heart Chakra including caretaking (*with agenda*); shame and not receiving support. The inner critic, feelings of unworthiness and perfectionism are all issues guided by shame. You may tend to by-pass the feelings you carry in your heart chakra and, instead, live in your head by intellectualizing, rationalizing and judging.

Earlier I talked about the heart being the residential choice of the inner child. I will say a few words here about the inner child which is a concept that has its roots in ancient mythologies and religions. Some of the examples of the *lost child as divine leader* are Moses, Jesus and Buddha.

KEEPING IT SIMPLE

Carl Jung talks about the archetypical *divine child.*

Eric Berne, father of *transactional analysis,* discusses the aspects of parent, adult and child within each of us.

John Bradshaw and Charles Whitfield popularized this concept of the inner child as a movement.

Basically the *inner child* is the child that you once were and the child that you remain regardless of your chronological age. In childhood, even when one is fortunate to grow up in a wonderful home, the child is wounded.

Why?

Because before you attained the age of approximately seven you had not reached what is termed the *age of reason*. As a young child you absorbed everything and everyone around you like a sponge, through your feelings and your emotions. Because you did not have the ability to reason you relied on your feelings and emotions to define who you are and your place in the world.

Even in the best of homes a child's feelings are hurt and wounded.

In a dysfunctional home a child's feelings are deeply hurt and deeply wounded. If this was your experience than as you grew into adulthood you carried the hurts of childhood along with you. Usually your wounds were hidden somewhere deep within your body.

As a psychospiritual therapist, using the tool of guided visualization, I have worked with clients who found their inner child hiding in their Base Chakra, their Solar Plexus energy centre or up in their heads.

Once you meet your inner child, wherever you may discover her, you will be able, through guided visualization, to bring the *child* into the heart where the *adult* allows the *parent within* to nurture, comfort and heal the *child within.*

Once you have done this then you, the adult, promise the child that you will take charge of his life and stop sending the *child to do the man's work.* The heart is truly the home of the inner child. In this chakra you are able to offer the child unconditional love, support and guidance that was too often lacking in the child's human experience.

There are many emotional issues associated with the Heart Chakra.

KEEPING IT SIMPLE

Meditation, with the focus on this energy centre, will allow you to recognize and gain insight into these issues. Should you choose to pursue the healing of these issues through psychospiritual therapy, the healing process begins.

Some of the emotional issues associated with the heart chakra include:

> Caretaking (with agenda)
>
> Feeling unsupported
>
> Feeling shame
>
> Feeling not good enough (inner critic)
>
> Perfectionism.

Keep in mind that issues of the *inner critic* and *perfectionism* are guided by *shame*.

These are issues that you may choose to ignore possibly because you are afraid to re-experience painful feelings and memories. Instead you may choose to by-pass the heart. The result of this by-pass is an individual who lives in his head; one who intellectualizes, rationalizes and judges his feelings and the feelings of others rather than allowing himself to *feel feelings* and to *have empathy* for the feelings of others.

KEEPING IT SIMPLE

Below is a list of emotional issues associated with the Heart Chakra.

Caretaking (with agenda)

Feeling unsupported

The inner critic

Perfectionism

And now I will go into more depth on each of the issues.

CARETAKING WITH AGENDA

Unlike the behaviour of a powermonger, the actions of one who needs to caretake others (*with agenda*) do not display one who is an obvious abuser. It is possible, in fact, that appearance-wise; this individual can often be wrongly described as one who is giving, and caring about the needs of others. You may even know someone just like this who has to have her finger in every pie. She is one who anticipates the needs of others and meets them before they have the opportunity to recognize they have a need.

He may be the one who serves on every committee; always giving, giving, giving of his time and energy. This person literally gives until it hurts.

And, in fact, it does hurt both the giver and the receiver.

Why?

KEEPING IT SIMPLE

Well, this individual who is so very generous of his time and energy is subconsciously giving in order to feel needed. And by feeling needed, almost indispensable, he tries to hold others to him. He wants to control their lives in such a way that they will need him so much that they will never leave or abandon him.

The *caretaker with agenda* wants to take care of everyone.

What she may or may not realize is that by attempting to take care of everyone and everything she is depriving others of their own powers of decision-making and action. She wants to feel appreciated and is often surprised when she isn't. And when she does not feel appreciated, sometimes not even a thank-you for all her efforts then resentment and anger builds within her.

KEEPING IT SIMPLE

Let's face it; the only people who need to be taken care of are children, sick people and sometimes the elderly.

It is desirable to care about others and often it is difficult to discern the fine line between caring and taking care. Someone who feels the need to take care of others is a controlling individual who lacks self-control and self-love.

He is the one who feels not good enough to just be who he is. She feels she has to take care of others because if she does not, she fears others will not want to be with her.

Caretaking is a fearful, controlling expression of insecurity and low self-esteem.

Perhaps you have met someone with caretaking issues. Perhaps you have heard him say, *"After all I've done for you, why don't you love me? Why don't you want me in your life?"*

Unaware of the subtle abuse they are heaping onto the unwilling recipient of all this caretaking, she cannot understand why she is not appreciated, *"after all I have done and sacrificed for you."*

Those with this emotional issue are unaware that they are depriving others of the right and privilege to take care of themselves in their own way and in their own time.

Through healing meditation focused on the heart chakra and further, through the process of psychospiritual therapy, one can work through these issues of caretaking with agenda. It is possible to understand the distinction between caretaking and caring about. And with this new understanding there is little fear that one will *throw out the baby with the bath water.* In other words it is possible to avoid the extreme polarization and become one who does not care at all. The middle road is the desirable path to discover and along this path one can learn to express love by a willingness to let go and allow others to find their own way.

FEELING UNSUPPORTED

If you felt unsupported during childhood chances are these feelings have been carried into adulthood. And this *feeling of being unsupported in adulthood* may or may not reflect the actuality of the support you are receiving from others in your adult life experience.

In other words, it is possible to, indeed, have the emotional support of others yet not *feel* this support. Conversely, it is possible to not have the actual emotional support of others in life yet our need for this feeling of support is great enough that we do not allow ourselves to see the actuality of no emotional support from others.

I know that may have sounded a bit confusing. And to have those feelings is also very bewildering. The reason for this confusion can be that you have not

KEEPING IT SIMPLE

learned to identify your needs and also you have not learned to express your needs. Instead you simply assume that others should know what your needs are. You may feel that it should not be necessary for you to express your needs in order to discover if your significant other is able or willing to meet them.

When I was in private practice I often had clients who would say, *"He doesn't do anything to support me. I feel all alone in this situation."*

And I ask the question, *"Have you expressed to your significant other that you need his support and help?"*

Invariably the answer is, *"No. If he/she loves me I shouldn't have to ask for help and support. He/she should be able to see that I need it."*

This inability to ask to have needs met is often the crux of the problem and the source of one's feelings of being unsupported. Most often a person with this issue did not feel safe enough in childhood to ask to have needs met and this *unsafe* feeling has been carried into adulthood.

This person possibly feels as though he carries the burdens of the world on his shoulders and he will often suffer from upper back pain, shoulder pain, angina or other heart ailments.

If you are someone who feels unsupported you will often unconsciously choose a partner in life who is either unable or unwilling to offer support simply because you are comfortable and *at home* with this feeling even though the niggling discomfort with this sense of *comfortableness* often surfaces throughout the experience of day to day living. You may often walk with your head down; shoulders slumped giving the appearance of someone who is barely able to support himself.

KEEPING IT SIMPLE

Through quiet meditation you can meet your inner self and you can recognize your inner feelings of being unsupported. By acting on this recognition by continued meditation and, if you choose, working through this issue in psychospiritual therapy, you can learn the emotional source of this issue. By trusting your therapeutic process you will learn to trust yourself.

Learning to trust you will open new doorways and these feelings of being unsupported can be transformed into a *knowing* that it is okay to have needs. It is okay to have needs met.

You may further discover that you are capable of meeting many of these needs by yourself for yourself. Rather than feeling depressed because you need to do this for yourself you will begin to feel confident and good that you are capable of doing this for yourself.

KEEPING IT SIMPLE

Once you learn to be self-supporting, you will learn that it is possible you can become strong enough for others to reach out to you, to express their needs to you and, *wonder of wonders*, you will discover that you are emotionally strong enough to not only be there for yourself but for others as well.

THE INNER CRITIC

This heart chakra issue expresses itself and gives a person the message, *I am not good enough.*

The inner critic is that aspect of you that makes an entrance in the early years of childhood. Some of the negative messages sent by parents, teachers, and other authority figures in a child's life might include: *You are not good enough* or *You are stupid* or *What makes you think you are capable of doing something like that?*

Hurting comments such as these are absorbed like a sponge into the essence of a child. In his earliest years the child is shamed.

And what happens when this childhood wound is not nurtured and healed is that it is carried into adulthood. Even though there may be no one sending these negative messages to you, the message is always being sent. And who is sending the message?

The inner critic, of course! Eric Berne, father of transactional analysis, may call this inner critic the *critical parent within.*

This inner critic does everything in its power to sabotage you. It is the inner critic, based in fear, who tells you that you are not going to win so there is no point in even entering the race. It is the inner critic who will find something negative to say about any achievement --- it is never good enough. *Nothing ever satisfies the critic within.*

Meditating with the focus on the heart chakra will allow you to get in touch with this inner critic. Through continued meditation and, if you choose, through psychospiritual therapy, it is possible for you to discover the source of the inner critic. It is possible to understand why the inner critic made its debut. It is also possible to honour, acknowledge and even to thank the inner critic for all that it attempted to do in order to protect you.

And it is within the realm of possibility that you can transform the inner critic, the critical parent within, into the *nurturing parent within*.

You can learn to parent yourself; to offer the love, the trust and the confidence that you never received in your early childhood period.

PERFECTIONISM

Similar to the emotional issue of not being good enough, the issue of perfectionism is one that centres in the heart chakra.

And what is a perfectionist?

A perfectionist is one who is extremely demanding on self and others to be something that is an impossible achievement for any human being. That *something* is the need to be perfect.

A human being is far from perfect. Perhaps one is perfect in the eyes of God but only God is perfect and however much one loves God, one will never be God and one will never be perfect.

And a perfectionist, in his mind, knows he will never be perfect.

However, in his heart, he forever strives to be the impossible; the perfect human being with the perfect life, the perfect relationship, the perfect family, the perfect profession and the perfect home.

Perhaps you have met a perfectionist. Perhaps you are one. It is difficult to feel comfortable in the home of a perfectionist. Imagine how uncomfortable it must feel to live in the human body of a perfectionist.

The polarity of the perfectionist is *the slob*. The slob is the one whose life is in utter chaos. He may be the bum on the park bench with the bottle of wine. He is seldom recognized as a perfectionist but he could very well be one just the same.

A slob is a perfectionist who gave up; who stopped trying to be perfect.

The slob and the perfectionist are opposite sides of the same coin and neither are happy campers.

KEEPING IT SIMPLE

Through meditation with the focus on your heart chakra you can meet the perfectionist within. You can dialogue and learn to understand the origin of this sub-personality within you. Once you have met you can, through continued meditation and, if you choose, by working through this issue in psychospiritual therapy, transform the perfectionist/slob into a well-balanced person who is able to accept shortcomings and limitations while recognizing your abilities and strengths. You can find this capability within yourself and literally tell the perfectionist/slob to *take a hike*.

SUMMARY

In summary, the heart chakra is the place where heaven and earth meet. It is the home of unconditional love. This is where you carry your grief, your sorrow and much emotional pain. But this is also where you find the love that heals; the love that overcomes; the love that sustains and nurtures.

If you by-pass the heart and resort instead to intellectualizing, rationalizing and judging your feelings rather than feeling your feelings then, in my view, you are short-changing yourself. You are underestimating the power of the love that is not far; the power of the love that is within your own heart just waiting to be accepted.

A meditation for the Heart Chakra follows.

■■■

MEDITATION

FOR THE HEART CHAKRA

Relax as you sit with your hands on your knees, palms upward to receive. Close your eyes. Breathe deeply. Allow the cares and the worries of your day to evaporate as though they had never existed. You are here; present in the moment. Allow your body and your mind to be still.

Place your hand over your heart chakra. Feel its loving energy. Stay with these feelings of love.

Now imagine a portal opening above you in the centre of the room. See streams of white light pouring through this portal. Allow this divine, creative, healing light to enfold you in its warmth.

Invite the white light to enter your body beginning at your feet. Feel it travel up through your legs, through your base chakra, through your sacral chakra, through your solar plexus chakra to your heart chakra. Within this energy centre is where unconditional love rests. Its element is air and its colour is pink or green.

See your heart chakra open and receptive. Visualize the release of the brilliant pink or green. See this colour merge with the powerful white light. Your heart chakra is filled with white and pink or white and green, blending, separating and merging together.

Now visualize this pink or green emanating from your heart. Feel the loving energy fill the room. See the room filled with rays of pink or green light and feel the powerful energy as you give and receive love within yourself.

KEEPING IT SIMPLE

Now allow the healing white light to fill your heart chakra and affirm unconditional self-love. Allow yourself to receive the following affirmations.

I focus on my heart where heaven and earth meet in harmony. I love myself and this love within me I share with others in my world. I am able to give and receive love. I give positive strokes to myself, recognizing my limitations and loving my strengths.

The child within me is bathed in unconditional love knowing I am there to give comfort. I affirm the child. I parent the child. I play with the child and promise to meet the needs of the innocent, loving child within me.

And now see the portal above you with white rays of loving energy flowing down and enveloping you. Feel the love of your highest self fill your heart. Feel the love of your higher power fill your heart.

Connect to the light. Allow it to flow through you and fill your heart centre until you are one with the light. Feel the loving, healing rays of white light. Stay with the love.

Silent meditation for five minutes…….

Now see the portal above you closing. Close and seal your heart chakra with love. Prepare yourself to return to the room. Feel your feet grounded solid on the floor. Send grounding rods deep within the earth ensuring your sense of centredness and balance.

When you feel ready, open your eyes.

***

THROAT CHAKRA

Throat Chakra

Located in your throat and extending throughout the tongue, your mouth, your arms and hands, the throat chakra is associated with the colour sky blue. Its element is sound. This energy centre is the centre of your creativity. In the beginning there was *the word* and from the word were all things created.

The throat chakra is the energy centre which controls your ability to express feelings, beliefs and attitudes. It is from here that you discover you are able to speak up and have a voice. You have something important to say and your throat chakra is the centre of this recognition and acceptance.

Your creativity is centred in this energy centre and it is here that you will also find your self-expression and creative problem-solving ability.

It is through the throat chakra that you connect with your Higher Power via the word and by prayer. Here you discover your connection with your Higher Power and your gifts of inspirational speaking and writing.

There are many emotional issues that, until resolved, have the power to block the throat chakra.

KEEPING IT SIMPLE

These issues include:

Having no voice,

Not expressing feelings.

Being unable to ask to get your needs met.

When a person polarizes he will talk incessantly. He will rarely listen to what his inner self or others may have to say to him. He may not honour his creativity or, in the extreme, he may develop a grandiosity often found present in a creative prima Dona.

Though this energy centre is located in the area of the throat its powerful energy extends to the tongue, the mouth, the arms and the hands. It is from here that the speaker, the actor, the painter, the singer, the musician, and the writer draw their creative gift.

KEEPING IT SIMPLE

When these artists accept the gift of their talent they will appreciate the free-flowing energy of their throat chakra.

However when these creative people find themselves stuck in their work and unable to express, to paint, to sing, to play, or to write, it is because they are experiencing an emotional block in their throat chakra. No doubt you have heard of writers' block and now you have a clearer understanding of why these blocks occur.

This energy centre is the one from which you experience self-expression. When you are being all that you can be; expressing all that you are; going with the flow of energy and honouring your creativity then you experience fulfillment and peace of mind. This honouring of creativity extends to your ability to creatively solve life problems and meet life challenges.

The throat chakra is also your connection to your Higher Power, your God as you conceive God to be. It is here that you will discover your innate gifts of spiritual speaking and spiritual writing.

When you meditate with the focus on your throat chakra and when you allow the connection to your Higher Power to be open and clear then you have access to the greatest wisdom and you can transmit this wisdom through the throat chakra in the form of speaking or writing. You merely need to be open and receptive. Just listen and transcribe.

It is quite simple but it is important to keep in mind that it is not always easy to be simple. But it is possible that with the help of your Higher Power you can co-create your reality.

There are many emotional issues associated with the throat chakra. If your throat chakra is blocked it could possibly be because one or more of the following issues have yet to be recognized, honoured and worked through by you.

This recognition and honouring is one aspect of meditation with the focus on the throat chakra. And this working through of issues is an opportunity offered to the meditation practitioner in the psychospiritual therapeutic process should he choose to pursue this path of personal self-discovery and personal growth.

Some emotional issues associated with this energy centre include:

Having No Voice

Not Expressing Feelings

Unable to Ask to Get Needs Met

Excessive Talking

Not Honouring Creativity

KEEPING IT SIMPLE

And now I will go into each of these issues in a little more depth.

HAVING NO VOICE

What does it mean to have no voice? More important, how does it feel to have no voice?

To have no voice could mean one of many things. A person with no voice may be one whose belief system was inherited from a parent or guardian whose philosophy was, *Children are to be seen but not heard.*

A person with no voice may be one who, as a child, often heard the brutal words, *Shut up!*

And this adult with no voice will be one who rarely speaks and when he does, he will speak in soft tones, hesitant and often his words will be apologetic. For example, he may say, *I'm probably wrong but .....* Or *I shouldn't say anything but ....*

And how might it be to be a person with no voice? There is possibly a feeling or a desire to be invisible because as a child he learned to *behave as though he were invisible; not seen or heard.*

By focusing on the throat chakra in meditation you can discover this unconscious desire to be neither seen nor heard. And understanding that this emotion is based in fear it is possible through further affirmative meditation on the throat chakra and, if you choose, by entering into the healing process of psychospiritual therapy, to rediscover your voice. It is possible that you do, indeed, have something to say and you may learn that what you have to say is very important.

NOT EXPRESSING FEELINGS

This emotional issue is another associated with the throat energy centre. If this issue is one that you recognize in yourself you know that when you allow yourself to feel feelings you undergo a frightening experience. To express the feelings you have allowed yourself to feel is an even more frightening experience because what will be the consequences?

What were the consequences in childhood?

As a child, when you expressed the emotion of anger, were your feelings of anger acknowledged and honoured? Or were you reprimanded, disciplined, punished or perhaps abused?

As a child, when you expressed the emotion of tearful sadness were your feelings of sadness acknowledged, honoured and nurtured or were you told *boys don't cry* or did you hear the painful words, *Cry baby! Cry baby!*

And even as a child, when you expressed the emotion of joy, were your feelings of exuberance and happiness encouraged or were you warned, *Don't get too excited! You will only end up crying!*

Throughout many homes in our western society children are taught that it is good to *repress* and *deny feelings.* Consequently these children learn to be afraid of their own feelings, in particular those feelings which have sadly earned a bad reputation such as *anger, fear and sadness*.

How difficult it is for such people to grow into adulthood only to discover that there are those of us who not only request but need a partner in relationship who is able to openly, safely express feelings and emotions.

KEEPING IT SIMPLE

By focusing on the throat chakra in meditation you are able to become aware of your own fear and inability to express emotion. Through continued affirmative meditation and, if you choose, by working through the childhood origins of this issue, it is possible for you to make acquaintance with these feelings that have been long bottled up and repressed.

It is possible, having made their acquaintance, to learn new and safe ways to express these feelings. In so doing you will feel free to express who you are.

UNABLE TO GET NEEDS MET

I have addressed this issue somewhat in discussion of the emotional issue of *feeling unsupported* in relation to the *Heart Chakra*. Putting the focus on the throat chakra, it is possible that an individual has some awareness of his needs but the fear remains. The fear is in expressing needs and asking another to meet those needs.

This is another example of someone who in early childhood developed a belief system that *no one is interested in or able or willing to meet my needs.* Therefore, early in life, this child learned to swallow the expression of his needs and he learned how to store them away deep inside.

Sometimes an individual stores his needs deep, deep inside with the result that he develops the belief that he has no needs. Or, if he is in touch with his needs, he develops the belief that the needs of others are more important than his own.

By focusing on the throat chakra in meditation this person is able to become aware of his need to ask to get needs met. With this new awareness, if he chooses, he is able to learn through the process of psychospiritual therapy how to overcome his fear.

If you feel this is a description of you, please remember it is possible to learn that your needs are valid and important. It is possible to learn that it is okay to ask for the help of another in order to have these needs met.

EXCESSIVE TALKING

Another emotional issue associated with the energy centre in the area of the throat is *excessive talking*. This is the polarity or the opposite side of the same coin called *having no voice*.

An individual who has no voice cannot be heard. An individual who talks excessively cannot be heard.

He can't be heard because others learn to *tune him out*.

NOT HONOURING CREATIVITY

Another emotional block of the throat chakra may be termed *not honouring creativity*. Everyone is blessed with a unique talent and creative gifts. To believe this is to achieve this.

This seems, even to me, like a simple remedy and I am once more reminded that it is not always easy to be simple.

The polarity of *not honouring creativity* could be termed an individual whose behaviour is *grandiose.*

To be grandiose means to be bigger than life; to be full of yourself; a veritable Prima Dona.

Through quiet meditation focusing on the throat chakra it is possible for this person to become aware of his grandiosity. Once aware, it is possible through continued affirmative meditation and, if he chooses, through psychospiritual therapy, to learn not only that it is okay, even positive, to honour one's creativity but also that it is possible to learn humility, confidence and to have a comfortable acceptance of your creativity without feeling the need to be what others may term conceited or grandiose.

You can learn the distinction between being centred in self and self-centredness.

Rather than keeping others at a distance by boasting and bragging you can, by maintaining an assertive self-confidence in your creativity, draw others into your life who will respect and honour your creative expression. Through this energy centre one co-creates his reality.

If you want to know where you are going in life, take a look at where you've been. If you like where you've been, keep on doing what you have been doing.

KEEPING IT SIMPLE

If you don't like where you've been, consider the possibility of transforming your life through positive affirmative meditation and through the process of psychospiritual therapy. You can change the direction your life has been taking.

In the beginning there was the word. The word, *the voice*, is situate in the throat chakra and is the centre of your creativity. A meditation for the Throat Chakra follows.

***

KEEPING IT SIMPLE

MEDITATION

FOR THE THROAT CHAKRA

Relax as you sit with your hands on your knees, palms upward to receive. Close your eyes. Breathe deeply. Allow the cares and the worries of your day to evaporate as though they had never existed. You are here; present in the moment. Allow your body and your mind to be still.

Imagine a portal opening above you. See streams of white light pouring through this portal. Allow this divine, creative, healing white light to enfold you in its warmth.

Invite the light to enter your body beginning at your feet. Feel it travel up through your legs, through your base chakra, your sacral chakra, through your solar plexus chakra and your heart chakra, to your throat chakra.

KEEPING IT SIMPLE

This energy centre is associated with communication and having a voice. Its element is sound and its colour is sky blue.

Open your throat chakra. See it open and receptive. Visualize the release of the beautiful sky blue and see this blue light merge with the white light. Imagine your throat chakra is filled with white and blue; blending, separating and merging together.

Allow the healing white light to fill your throat chakra. Affirm your personal power with confidence and love. Affirm your own voice. Allow yourself to accept the following affirmations.

I communicate with ease and clarity. I have a voice and I am able to speak up for myself. I recognize the importance of what I have to say and I know others will benefit by listening to me. I express myself with confidence and love. And my connection to my Higher Power assures me I can experience spiritual speaking.

Now open your mouth and activate your voice. Hear yourself expressing the sound, *OHM,* and affirm; *When I express OHM, I express my feelings. When I express OHM I discover that I can voice my needs and get them met. When I express OHM I am reminded that I need not talk excessively. It is unnecessary because when I speak I am clear in my expression. I am heard. I find my voice when I express OHM. The healing white light fills my throat and I express OHM.*

Now see the portal above you closing. Close and seal your throat chakra with love. Prepare yourself to return to the room. Feel your feet grounded solid on the floor. Send grounding rods deep into the earth and this will ensure your sense of centredness and balance within your being. When you feel ready, open your eyes.

BROW CHAKRA

Brow Chakra

The brow chakra, sometimes called the *Third Eye* is located in the centre of your forehead and the colour associated with this energy centre is indigo. Its element is light.

When one considers the meaning of *light* in a spiritual sense one would describe it as enlightenment.

KEEPING IT SIMPLE

Jesus has been quoted as saying, *"My burden is light."* Buddha suggests that you *"be your own light."*

Each year those of the Hindu faith celebrate Deepavali or the Festival of Lights while those of the Jewish faith celebrate Chanukah with the lighting of the Menorah.

When I was a child in Sunday School we would sing the lyrics, *This little light of mine, I'm going to let it shine. Hide it under a bushel? No, I'm going to let it shine, let it shine, let it shine.*

The wisdom of the ancients teaches us to always let our light shine.

The element of the brow chakra is light and when this energy centre is open and the energy is free-flowing you shine in your own light. Your imagination is vivid; your ability to visualize is sharpened and you will experience mental clarity.

The brow chakra is the centre of your intuition. From here you are able to sense a feeling within that lets you know what others are feeling or thinking. It is from here that you are able to *tune in to others.*

Clairvoyance means clear vision about your life's purpose and during meditation, if your focus is on your brow chakra, your gift of clairvoyance will be sharpened. It is possible that you may receive messages through imagery.

Through this energy centre it is also possible to develop an ability to actually see the energy field surrounding an individual. This energy field is called the aura.

From this centre you can discover and develop your psychic abilities. You may be able to visualize things which are not readily seen in the physical realm. By developing your brow chakra you will be able to have an understanding of those things that often seem to be beyond understanding.

There are many emotional issues associated with the brow chakra. Some of them include: (a) Over-use of mental defenses; sometimes to the point of dissociation.

(b) Avoiding introspection and self-examination which leaves you always looking for the answer, the solution or the understanding in all the wrong places. In other words you will be looking everywhere but within yourself.

By not developing the brow chakra you will live unconsciously remaining unaware of your true potential. To experience *conscious living* I encourage you to develop the gifts revealed to you through your brow chakra.

This energy centre is also associated with your physical eyesight; your ability to see with clarity. There is also an association with your ears and your ability to hear without impediment.

You have sometimes said to someone or, indeed, someone may have at one time or another said to you, *"You hear what you want to hear"* or *"You only see what you want to see."*

There is much truth in these statements. It is true that emotional blocks in the brow chakra can manifest physically in poor eyesight or hearing loss.

It is possible through meditation focused on this energy centre to discover these emotional blocks and, further, it is possible that if you choose to work through these emotional issues in psychospiritual therapy you can improve your physical vision and hearing.

KEEPING IT SIMPLE

As in all things it is recommended that a student of this type of higher learning remain grounded and centred in self. I say this because there can be some danger of an individual going to an extreme in developing his psychic abilities where he may find himself avoiding the reality of the human experience or, in other words, living in fantasy.

When a student places all of his focus on the spiritual chakras in meditation and avoids the emotional issues of the lower chakras including the base, sacral and solar plexus energy centres, he may discover that he is doing what is commonly termed *a spiritual bypass*.

This person may not be aware he is doing this because he has become too out of touch with his own human emotional issues.

KEEPING IT SIMPLE

It is important when you step onto the path of meditation to ensure groundedness, centredness and an awareness of all aspects of your human being including body, mind and spirit. In this way you will be able to achieve a healthy physical, emotional, mental and spiritual balance within.

I caution all students of meditation to strive for, develop and maintain this healthy balance in order to avoid falling into what is sometimes called *The New Age Airhead Syndrome.*

While meditating it is possible to visit the higher realms of the heavens, so to speak, but it is recommended that you do this with your *feet on the ground*. Meditation is a wonderful tool which will aid you in improving your human experience.

If mis-used, meditation can be a doorway to one's avoidance of the human experience and one's avoidance of the responsibilities and joys inherent in the experience of being a human being.

Spiritual and emotional awareness is a gift but it does come with a price tag. Is it possible this is why Jesus termed *light* a *burden*? Awareness, on its own, can lead one to live in a *fantasy land*.

A key to a well balanced life is *awareness plus acceptance plus action* which will equal transformational change in a person who is willing to trust his process in psychospiritual therapy.

Some of the emotional issues associated with the Brow Chakra include:

    Denial

    Over-use of mental defenses

    Avoiding introspection

KEEPING IT SIMPLE

By-passing the heart and staying in the head

Avoiding reality

And now I will discuss each of these emotional issues in a little more depth.

DENIAL

A good place to start is to ask the question, *What is denial?*

When you have not developed your awareness of who you are; your connectedness to others and your place in the world in which you find yourself living, then you will be like the proverbial ostrich with your head stuck in the sand.

You will find that your life is happening to you as opposed to you making things happen.

To be in denial is to live unconsciously; to not recognize and accept responsibility for your thoughts, words or actions. You will most likely be a person who is often surprised when things don't happen the way you may have hoped and yet you will believe and probably say, *"I'm fine. I just have the worst luck!"* or

"I'm fine. I just happen to meet the wrong people," or *"I'm fine but everyone else has a problem."*

This individual is experiencing absolute powerlessness but is in such denial he does not even recognize that he is powerless. A person living in denial lives unconsciously.

Most often it will take a major life crisis in this person's life to *hammer him on the head*, so to speak, and wake him up to the realization that he is in need of help. There are those of us who will receive many *hammers on the head* before the impact of the hammer is sufficient to alert us that it is time to wake up and live consciously.

OVER-USE OF MENTAL DEFENSES

The over-use of mental defenses is similar to denial although usually the consequences of this defense are not as clearly obvious as those of denial.

An extreme example of the over-use of mental defenses would be an individual who has dissociated from himself and others.

A more moderate example of someone who over-uses his mental defenses will be one who, rather than feeling his feelings, will justify, rationalize or intellectualize. This person may be quite qualified to *talk the talk* but by avoiding his feelings, his body and his emotional issues, he will be quite incompetent when it comes to *walking the walk*.

In fact, in an extreme case, a person may find himself with physical injury to his feet, ankles, knees or legs. These are all body parts associated with the base chakra; thus a physical manifestation of his inability to walk the emotional and spiritual path.

It is possible through guided meditation and, if one chooses, through psychospiritual therapy to overcome the fear associated with feeling feelings. In doing so it is also possible for you to give your mind a rest for a change and to coin a phrase, *"Let me hear your talk"*.

Emotions live in your body.

Your head, all by itself, is incapable of feeling or expressing emotion. A person who *lives in his head* may talk with freedom about emotions but this same person will not allow himself to *feel his emotions.*

The element of the Brow Chakra is light. It is possible through meditation to shine the light on the over-use of mental defenses. It is also possible to

KEEPING IT SIMPLE

integrate body, mind, emotions and spirit in order to live a full, healthy, well-adjusted life.

AVOIDING INTROSPECTION

And SELF-EXAMINATION

Similar to the person who is in denial or the one who over-uses mental defenses, an individual who avoids introspection and self-examination is one who is out of touch with the totality of himself.

He is afraid to look within. There is, no doubt, good reason for this fear.

He is perhaps afraid to discover things about his life and himself that are less than pleasant. However a person who is fearful of visiting the *basement of his soul*, who is fearful of discovering what it really is that *makes him tick*, is one who also deprives himself of the wonderful gifts of creative potential that are also covered in the dust of the shadowy, buried, painful wounds of early childhood.

KEEPING IT SIMPLE

A very wise man once said, *"The answer is in the question."*

It is logical to assume that if one is fearful, unable or unwilling to go within to ask the questions one will never find the answers he is longing to know.

BY-PASSING THE HEART

Denial, over-use of mental defenses, avoiding introspection and self-examination, are all good examples of the emotional issues experienced by an individual who is by-passing the heart.

The heart chakra, the resting place of unconditional self-love, and the desired home of the inner child will remain blocked and as a consequence the Brow Chakra will also be blocked.

There can be no true understanding of self if one is not acquainted with his own feelings and emotions. If a person remains in his head where he can, with safety, rationalize, intellectualize and talk about feelings, his self-esteem will be low no matter how brilliant a mind he may have.

It is possible to become aware of this emotional issue in guided meditation. Further, for one who chooses, it is possible to break down the fearful barriers that keep the heart under lock and key. It is possible to integrate body, mind and spirit.

When you begin this process you will be on the road to physical, emotional and spiritual wellness. You will discover that you are much more than you ever *thought* you could be.

KEEPING IT SIMPLE

A SHORT SUMMARY

Of THE BROW CHAKRA

The brow chakra is the energy centre controlling your imagination, visualization, and mental clarity. Living in the information age this energy centre is often over-loaded with facts, figures, problems and mental solutions.

To live your life with an emotionally blocked Brow Chakra is to become like a computer; filled with knowledge and cold, hard facts.

By developing the Brow Chakra through guided meditation and psychospiritual therapy you will discover self-love along with a fuller sense of yourself and your life purpose. In becoming a more grounded, well-rounded person, not only will you like yourself a lot more but others will also find you more likeable. A meditation for the Brow Chakra follows.

KEEPING IT SIMPLE

MEDITATION

FOR THE BROW CHAKRA

Relax as you sit with your hands on your knees, palms upward to receive. Close your eyes. Breathe deeply. Allow the cares and the worries f your day to evaporate as though they had never existed. You are here, present in the moment. Allow your body and your mind to be still.

Imagine a portal above you in the centre of the room. Visualize streams of white light pouring through this portal. Allow this divine, creative, healing light to enfold you in its warmth.

Invite the light to enter your body beginning at your feet. Feel it travel up through your legs, through your base chakra, your sacral chakra, through your solar plexus chakra, your heart chakra and through your throat chakra to your Brow Chakra which is located in the centre of your forehead.

This energy centre is associated with imagination, mental clarity and the ability to visualize. Its element is light (enlightenment) and its colour is indigo.

Open your Brow Chakra. Release the brilliant indigo. See this indigo merge with the white light until your brow chakra is filled with white and indigo, blending, separating and merging together.

Now your brow chakra is open. Allow the healing white light to permeate your brow chakra and affirm your personal power with confidence and love. And now allow yourself to sink into your body, free your mind and totally relax as you enter a meditation of guided visualization.

KEEPING IT SIMPLE

Imagine you are in a forest. It is cool, comfortable and you are walking along a path. All around you is greenery and trees shimmering in the indigo light of the sky. You hear myriad bird songs and as you look up you catch glimpses of the sky not obliterated by the tall, green branches.

You feel very peaceful as you walk along this path but you have a curious mind which leads to a yearning to see more. You are in search of clarity which until now seems to have eluded you.

In the distance you hear the sound of a waterfall. You are drawn by this sound and quicken your pace just a little. You want to see this naturally flowing water. You know that somewhere within you there is the capacity to flow in this natural manner through life but too often the fear of self-examination has gotten your way.

KEEPING IT SIMPLE

But today in the forest you put this fear aside. You seek the awareness that is resting deep within. You say no to the temptation to deny this desire. You say no to the temptation to jump up into your head in order to justify or rationalize this desire. You allow your mind to be still and you simply keep walking until you reach the water's edge.

The waterfall is beautiful. Tremendous energy from high above you is rushing downward toward the river. You stand at the river's edge. At little distance down the shoreline you see a small boat.

You walk toward the boat and notice that it is a row boat.

You climb into the boat and take the oars into your hands. You are alone with your self, your higher self and your Higher Power. You are one with the free flowing river and you can choose whether you will stay at the shoreline or whether you will make use of the oars and join the river to go with the flow.

And now as you sit in the boat, oars in your hands, you look down and you are surprised to see that you are no longer an adult.

You are the seeking, loving, imaginative child that you remember once being a long, long time ago. You say hello to this child and allow her the opportunity to make the decision to move or to stay put. Be with the child and let him speak to you. Allow yourself to listen and simply be with this child. Let her take you through your memories and imagination to a place he wants to visit.

…silent meditation for 5 minutes…

Now it is time to leave the child. Invite him into your heart where it is warm and safe. Thank the child for touching and filling your heart with long-forgotten

KEEPING IT SIMPLE

emotions of joy and sorrow. You had forgotten that you had these gifts of clarity and emotion but the child is always there within you to remind you that creativity and imagination are yours to fulfill.

Again you look down and you see that you are no longer the child but the adult who carries the child in his heart. You are an adult sitting in the boat with the oars in your hands.

You begin to row toward shore. Once landed you get out of the boat and look again at the rushing waterfall, the free flowing river and somehow you know that you can visit this place again whenever you desire to get in touch with the child and the creative imagination within you.

Now retrace your steps through the forest and as you reach the edge of the forest you begin to prepare yourself to return to the room.

KEEPING IT SIMPLE

See the portal above you closing. Now close and seal your brow chakra with love. Feel your feet grounded solid on the floor. Visualize grounding rods deep within the earth ensuring your sense of centredness and balance.

When you feel ready, open your eyes.

***

CROWN CHAKRA

Crown Chakra

The Crown Chakra is located in the centre top of your head. Purple, the colour of royalty, is associated with this energy centre. Its element is thought. This chakra is the centre of your spiritual development and soul evolution. Through this centre you gain an understanding of your life's lessons and your higher purpose. It is here that you connect with the universe and experience a sense of oneness with all creation.

The Crown Chakra is your direct line to your Higher Power and it holds the awareness that we are each inter-connected. Here you can experience a unity of consciousness.

We associate this chakra with wisdom, higher knowledge and understanding. It is through the Crown Chakra that your higher self, spiritual self and your self-actualized self is able to be the observer and see the big picture of all that you are co-creating.

Some of the emotional issues associated with this chakra include:

Not trusting something greater than yourself and   Control issues that prevent you from surrendering to and trusting your own greatest wisdom and your own Higher Power

KEEPING IT SIMPLE

On the other hand, if you polarize and opt for a spiritual by-pass meaning you focus only on things spiritual without also doing your emotional inner work, this can create an imbalance in your life experience. If you were to compare yourself to a tree you will understand that the deeper the roots, the stronger the tree, the more beautiful and bountiful the leaves on the branches.

Addictions associated with the Crown Chakra are religious fanaticism and excessive meditation.

Spiritual awareness, without a solid base of good emotional well-being resulting in good physical well-being, will produce someone who will have a great deal of difficulty practicing what he preaches. And usually this type of sanctimonious individual will do a lot of self-righteous preaching. Basically he is the kind of person who will give the message, *Do what I say, not what I do.* The reason he gives this message is because without the solid foundation of a healthy emotional inner life resulting in a healthy physical life, he truly does not know how to do for himself what he quite ably instructs others to do.

To demonstrate this point let me share with you the following story shared with me by a dear friend.

A Poor Translation of a Rich Hindu Story

As told to me by Ishwardutt Sharma

The rich, well-dressed traveler was clumsy as he made his way into the boat. He was an over-weight, highly educated, self-righteous traveler who had some difficulty finding his footing before he plunked himself onto the soft-cushioned seat of the boat greatly disturbing the otherwise tranquil river's water. Had he taken the time to look up he would have noticed that the sky was an inspirational blue.

KEEPING IT SIMPLE

The boatman physically fit and swarthy, with calloused hands, dropped the oars into the water. Like a pebble in the pond the oars disturbed the stillness of the peaceful river, creating a ripple effect.

They were less than half-way across the river when the traveler decided to speak.

"Have you read the Gita, my good man?" he asked.

"No, sir," the boatman replied. "What is the Gita?"

"You don't know the Gita?" the traveler asked in amazement. "Are you not a Hindu?"

"Yes, sir," the boatman replied. "This is what I am told."

KEEPING IT SIMPLE

"You are a Hindu and you have not read the Gita? Have you read the Holy Book then and have you read of the wisdom of our ancestors?"

"I do not know how to read, sir," the boatman replied. "I come from a poor, humble family."

"If you do not know how to read, sir, then tell me this. Surely you have been told of the marvelous truth of the prophets?"

"I know only how to cross the river," the boatman responded.

Just then a strong wind tossed the boat. The sun disappeared behind the clouds and the rains began to fall.

The boatman asked the educated traveler, "Do you know how to swim, sir?"

KEEPING IT SIMPLE

"No, sir," the traveler replied. "I do not know how to swim."

With honest humility the boatman enquired, "Tell me, sir, in this treacherous weather, what good is all your knowledge if you do not know how to swim? As for me, sir, I do not require knowledge from books in order to know my God and myself. And as for me, sir," he shouted just before the boat capsized, "I do not need a boat to cross the river."

KEEPING IT SIMPLE

In summary, the Crown Chakra is the centre of your spiritual development and soul evolution. It is true that *man cannot live by bread alone.* It is equally true that *man cannot live without bread.*

To help you to experience your *self to the fullest, to be all that you can be,* through meditation and, if you choose, through psychospiritual therapy, you will learn the importance of the interconnectedness of all the chakras.

It is possible for you to be all that you can be; to reach your highest potential. The best example I can refer to is that set by Jesus who is often called *The All in All.* And it was He who is quoted as saying, "All these things I do, you can do also; even greater than these things."

A meditation for the Crown Chakra follows.

***

MEDITATION

FOR THE CROWN CHAKRA

Relax as you sit with your hands on your knees, palms upward to receive. Close your eyes. Breathe deeply. Allow the cares and the worries of your day to evaporate as though they had never existed. You are here, present in the moment. Allow your body and your mind to be still.

Imagine a portal opening above you in the centre of the room. See streams of white light pouring through this portal. Allow this divine, creative, healing white light to enfold you in its warmth. Invite the light to enter your body beginning at your feet. Feel it travel up through your legs, through your base chakra, your sacral chakra, through your solar plexus, your heart chakra, your throat chakra and through your brow chakra to your Crown Chakra which is centred on the top of your head. Allow your focus to stay on this energy centre because it is your connection to the universe, to your higher self and to God as you perceive God to be.

Open your Crown Chakra. See it open and receptive. Release the powerful purple and see the purple merge with the white light until your Crown Chakra is filled with white and purple, blending, separating, and merging together.

And now, filled with healing, white light, your Crown Chakra is open and receptive to your highest good. You feel one with your higher power and you affirm your connection to the universe. Feel the connection. Allow yourself to feel the love.

KEEPING IT SIMPLE

Now open your brow chakra; release the indigo.

Open your throat chakra; release the sky blue.

Open your heart chakra; release the pink or green.

Open your solar plexus chakra; release the yellow.

Open your sacral chakra; release the orange.

And, lastly, open your base chakra and release the red.

KEEPING IT SIMPLE

You are now open and receptive to your higher power. You are a rainbow of colour yet you are filled with the white, healing light.

Ask your higher self and ask your Higher Power, *What is your message for me?*

Affirm: *I am open, receptive and in the stillness, I hear. In the darkness, I see. I am here. I am listening for the quiet whisper of truth within me.*

Silent meditation for five minutes……

KEEPING IT SIMPLE

And now it is time to prepare to return to the room. See the portal above you closing. Beginning with your crown chakra, close this chakra and seal it with love. Close the brow chakra. Close the throat chakra, the heart chakra, the solar plexus, the sacral and the base chakra and seal them with love. Now all your chakras are closed. They are sealed with confidence and love. Know that the white light is never far. Know that the answers, the wisdom, and the love are never far. You need only seek the silence, look within and listen to the quiet whisper of truth within you.

Now feel your feet grounded solid on the floor. Send grounding rods deep within the earth ensuring your sense of centredness and balance within your being. When you feel ready; open your eyes.

***

IN SUMMARY

Throughout the process of writing this manuscript I have confirmed for myself that, although I have made my best attempt, it is not always easy to be simple. Nevertheless this has been my goal. Only you, the reader, can decide whether or not my goal was achieved.

In my lifetime I have discovered that Meditation is an introduction to the Chakra System and knowledge of the Chakra System is an invitation to experience Meditation.

Meditation and the Chakra System go hand in hand in forming an introduction to Psychospiritual Therapy which is reinforced by Meditation.

KEEPING IT SIMPLE

These three topics: *Meditation, the Chakra System and Psychospiritual Therapy* are a trinity. They form a perfect creation called a triangle or a *Merkaba,* if you will. A Merkaba is a vehicle that brings you, the seeker, out of darkness and into the light of a unified body, mind and spirit where you can reap the harvest of good health; emotional, mental, physical and spiritual.

You will discover that you can't have one without the other. You will also discover that it is possible to have it all. You can, in fact, be capable of creating in partnership with your Higher Power, *the all in all,* a fulfilling, healthy, peaceful and prosperous relationship with yourself and with all who are fortunate to meet you as you choose your steps along your path of personal growth and spiritual development called conscious living.

As a child in Sunday School I was taught a song. Some of the lyrics are, *Let Jesus come into your heart*..... In that same Sunday School, when asked where Jesus lived I responded *God is inside of me*. I was punished for that response. I was told that I should know better. I should know that Jesus lives in heaven. Hmmmm, even as a little girl I wondered why in this church they asked Jesus to come into their hearts in song if they did not believe He, the Divine, would ever live within a human being.

I live in hope. It is my hope that what I have written in these pages has been of interest and of value to you.

Let your light shine. God bless.

***

SOME REVIEWS OF

KEEPING IT SIMPLE

5.0 out of 5 stars A very easy-to-understand explanation of chakras
By Anu

This is a well written book - very easy to understand the concept of chakras and the significance of each chakra. I am yet to try out the exercises for opening up each chakra. But if you are looking to familiarize yourself with the 7 chakras of the Indian/yogic tradition, I highly recommend this book.

5.0 out of 5 stars It Really is Possible to Heal
By Mary Belanger

This manual is very well written which is to be expected of Audrey Austin who is a wonderful psychotherapy practitioner, author, and teacher.

I was introduced to Keeping it Simple in 2011. At that time I was chakra illiterate. I had no idea that seven major chakras existed.
The manuscript is put together in a very sequential manner. The reader is given a methodical overview of meditation, psychospiritual therapy, and the chakra system.

KEEPING IT SIMPLE

The straight forward approach on the practice of opening blocked chakras enables the reader to unite mind, body, and soul.

I have recorded the positive affirmations for each chakra. It is very comforting hearing my own voice as I meditate. I have been transformed into a healthier and happier person and am very grateful for Austin who has created such a wonderful resource on chakra meditation.

It really is possible to heal. Keeping it Simple has my Five Star rating because it has changed my life for the better.

OTHER BOOKS

BY AUDREY AUSTIN

Sara, a Canadian Saga

Reawakening

Ellen and The Hummingtree

The Silent Star Plus a Dozen

Moose Road – a Canadian Tragedy

Beyond The Blue

When God Gives Us Spring

Recompense

Social Studies – Book One –

   Dying To Be Popular

Social Studies – Book Two –

   Shattered and Broken

Social Studies – Book Three

   Weaving Alice

Audrey Austin's Author Page:

http://www.amazon.com/author/audreyaustin

http://www.facebook.com/audreyaustinca